W9-BUE-885

Wonderfully wise yet with sweet innocence, Marjorie Bottorff combines her own brand of humor with spiritual truths in these whimsical life-stories that will leave a lasting impression on your heart!

—Jane Hixon, parish nurse,
Kempsville Presbyterian Church,
Virginia Beach, VA

Bravo, Marjorie. This book is wonderful! Each delightful story delivers a powerful message and is an uplifting shot in the arm. You are incredibly talented. Please write more books. I want to give up real estate and be your manager!

—Trudy Hoff, RE/MAX Alliance,
Virginia Beach, VA

Simultaneously, Marjorie gives us gentle, sometimes wry humor, prophetic vision, and cherished moments; capturing the hearts of her readers, leaving them to ponder, 'Why didn't I think of that?' Once you are captured by one of her pearls, you find it nearly impossible not to go on to the next.

—Mike Rugless, retired captain, U.S. Navy

I truly laughed, and I honestly cried. The book is fantastic: poignant but not overwhelming! In today's increasing hustle and bustle, people need to start a book with the confidence that they will be able to finish it; this is just the concise and deeply moving relief we depend upon. Bright, real, and wonderful!

—Kathleen Hoff, University of Virginia

a String of PEARLS

Marjorie Ward Bottorff

a String of

PEARLS

Finding Humor in
Life's Daily Challenges

TATE PUBLISHING & Enterprises

A String of Pearls
Copyright © 2009 by Marjorie Ward Bottorff. All rights reserved.

No part of this publication may be reproduced, stored in a retrieval system or transmitted in any way by any means, electronic, mechanical, photocopy, recording or otherwise without the prior permission of the author except as provided by USA copyright law.

Unless otherwise noted, Scripture is taken from "NIV" Holy Bible, New International Version ®, Copyright © 1973, 1978, 1984 by International Bible Society. Used by permission of Zondervan Publishing House. All rights reserved.

Scripture quotations marked "NLT" are taken from the Holy Bible, New Living Translation, Copyright © 1996. Used by permission of Tyndale House Publishers, Inc. All rights reserved.

Scripture quotations marked "TLB" are taken from The Living Bible / Kenneth N. Taylor: Tyndale House, © Copyright 1997, 1971 by Tyndale House Publishers, Inc. Used by permission. All rights reserved.

The opinions expressed by the author are not necessarily those of Tate Publishing, LLC.

Published by Tate Publishing & Enterprises, LLC
127 E. Trade Center Terrace | Mustang, Oklahoma 73064 USA
1.888.361.9473 | www.tatepublishing.com

Tate Publishing is committed to excellence in the publishing industry. The company reflects the philosophy established by the founders, based on Psalm 68:11,
"The Lord gave the word and great was the company of those who published it."

Book design copyright © 2009 by Tate Publishing, LLC. All rights reserved.
Cover design by Amber Guliat
Interior design by Joey Garrett

Published in the United States of America

ISBN: 978-1-60696-980-9
1. Religion / Christian Life / Inspirational
2. Religion / Christian Life / Spiritual Growth
09.05.19

This is the field where, hidden, lies
The pearl of price unknown
That merchant is divinely wise
Who makes the pearl his own.

(Isaac Watts, "Laden With Guilt")

Dedication

I dedicate this book to David, my husband for forty-nine years. Thank you, David, for your constant support and encouragement. You are the love of my life.

Acknowledgments

If I acknowledged everyone who has been helpful, this page would be longer than the book. But I must thank a few. They are:

Donna Blackistone, who invited me to write a column for the monthly newsletter at Truro Church in Fairfax, Virginia, called *On the Light Side*—it was the beginning of this book.

Julie Lucas, who allowed me space on her website, which prompted me to continue writing. There is nothing like a deadline to make one productive.

Evelyn Wagoner, who provided a monthly home base that helped me to write better.

Julie Bottorff, Ginger Cage, Joy Cooley, and Lee Dumas, who understood the difference between critiquing and criticizing.

Ann Neidow, who so effortlessly solved my struggle for a title.

Rose Anne Conner, who reminded me so poignantly that God is not happy with those who hide their light under a bushel.

Tate Publishing, who treated this first-book-author as if she was important.

Table of Contents

Foreword

In one of his most familiar parables, Jesus compared the Kingdom of Heaven to the discovery of a pearl of great value. Recognition of that value and the willingness to pay the price to acquire it are the evidences of spiritual wisdom. The person who cannot tell the difference between a piece of costume jewelry and the real thing or the one who fails to recognize the worth of a good investment is destined to miss God's best.

Marjorie Bottorff has discovered not just a single gem of great value, but a whole string of pearls! I had the pleasure of being her pastor when she shared these pearls of wisdom in her monthly column, "On the Light Side," published in our parish newsletter.

Now, she has collected thirty-three pearls for daily reading. Her short meditations are marked by warmth, wit, and whimsy. And each will arrest, surprise, and delight you—and leave you hoping for more. In them you may see yourself, your circumstances, and God in new and wonderful ways.

—*The Right Rev. John W. Howe*
Episcopal Bishop of Central Florida
Orlando, Florida

Introduction

When asked what I do for a living, I answer, "I'm a kept woman, and my husband keeps me very well!" I say that because for most of our marriage I did not work outside of our home. I loved being a homemaker and a navy wife. Both roles kept me busy enough.

Through the years, many things happened to me that have been beyond my control. For example, where we moved and how often. The only choice I had was whether I would allow these things to make me better or bitter. *A String of Pearls* is primarily my reflection of some of the times that I have had to make that choice.

But whether an irritant was tough or funny, it marked my growing edge. And if I would let him, God would take that irritant and transform it into something lovely—in the same way an oyster makes a pearl.

A String of Pearls is a collection of articles that are independent of each other, like pearls on a necklace. The articles are strung together by humor. Usually they reflect my experience, like the article, "Be Not Anxious." Sometimes, however, they reflect my imagination, like the article, "CNN Interviews Mr. Noah."

You can read *A String of Pearls* any way you want, but I suggest that you read one a day—sort of like taking a spiritual vitamin. Sometimes they are more humorous than tough. Sometimes, however, they are more tough than humorous. But either way, I hope they make you laugh. And I hope they make you think.

I also hope that you will read this book because writers who have no one to read what they write are like musicians who have no one to listen to them, like toys that have no one to play with them. So come into my book and listen to the music and play with the toys. May the melody and the joy bless you!

—Marjorie Bottorff
Virginia Beach, VA

Be Not Anxious

If you don't mind my saying so, the Bible has some really absurd verses. In fact, one in particular, Philippians 4:6, strikes me as absolutely ridiculous. It's the verse that says, "Do not be anxious about anything."

Now, I can think of a number of things that any sensible person ought to be anxious about. Let me give one example of something that I thought deserved a lot of anxiety. In graduate school, I was preparing to do a session of practice teaching. My subject was the book of Daniel; my audience was seventy-five college students; I was using a microphone for the first time; I was using an overhead projector for the first time; the class would last for one full hour; and my professor was sitting in the front row.

I could see a lot in that situation to be anxious about. In fact, I thought that everything in that situation deserved anxiety. So the Lord and I had this discussion: "Lord, you can't be serious about my not being anxious about this." He assured me that he was.

"But, Lord, there's a grave risk of failure here, and you know how I avoid even the slightest possibility of failure." He assured me that he knew that too.

Then something lovely happened. He showed me how he views what we call failure. He reminded me of my children learning to walk. They would take a step and fall down. Then they would get back up and fall again, and get back up and fall again. Yet never once did it enter my mind to say, "You dummy. You fell down again. Why don't you just quit?" Never! Parents are meant to be encouragers. "Good try. Now get back up and try again. That's it. You're learning."

"The reason you fear failure," the Lord said, "is because of how it makes you feel about yourself. You say to yourself, 'You dummy. You fell again. Why don't you just give up?' But I say to you, Good try. Now get back up and try again. That's it; you're learning."

In other words, to God, failure is not falling down; failure is staying down. Martin Luther acknowledged this when he wrote that the first ten years of a Christian's life are spent learning how to get back up again.

Lord, help us to see our failures through Calvary. At Calvary, the world saw an empty cross whose dead victim was lying in a tomb; they called it failure.

But God knew that his Son wouldn't stay down; God called it victory!

Guess Who's Coming to Dinner

There is all the difference in the world between knowing someone and knowing about someone. For example, if you read the paper or watch the news, you know a lot about our president. You know about his family, about his politics, and even about his religion. But unless you've met him face to face and have spent time with him, you don't know him.

The difference between the two made such a deep impression on me that I was stunned when my friend said to me some years ago, "Marjorie, you know a lot about Jesus, but do you know him?"

It did not take long for me to answer, "No, I don't; but I'd like to." Then she reminded me of his promise in Revelation 3:20, "Here I am! I stand at the door and knock. If anyone hears my voice and opens the door, I will come in and eat with him, and he with me."

Well, I thought, *if Jesus is coming to dinner, I had better get ready*. Being the good housewife that I am, my first thought was to clean house; but much to my distress, the more I tried to clean, the more mess I uncovered.

Leaving that idea behind, I went to prepare dinner and was once again distressed when I realized that the pantry was bare. I had nothing to offer him. I was embarrassed for Jesus to find my house in such a mess with no dinner to offer him.

Nevertheless, I opened the door and invited him to come in. It was the best decision I ever made as I discovered that he had not come to be my guest; he had come to be my friend. He had not come to inspect my house; he had come to clean it. And he had not come to be served; he had come to serve. As for no food on the table, Jesus said, "I am the bread of life. He who comes to me will never go hungry, and he who believes in me will never be thirsty" (John 6:35). I was glad he had not come to visit, but to stay.

May I ask you the same question? Do you know Jesus, or do you just know about him? If you don't yet know him, then he's still knocking at your door. But he will not come in until you open it.

Please don't wait too long. The danger isn't that he will stop knocking. The danger is that you will stop listening.

A Thought for the Day

Computers are predictable.
God is not.

Computers come in boxes.
God is always outside the box.

Computers can be repaired.
God never breaks.

Computers become outdated and are replaced.
God never gets outdated. He is irreplaceable.

Computers can be programmed to do what we want.
Don't even think about it!

Computers know a lot about the universe.
God knows everything about the universe.
He created it, including you and me.

I wonder what would happen if we spent as much time with God as we spend with our computers.

Our Three Thousand Mile Obstacle Course

As a navy family we moved from coast to coast often. One of our more memorable trips was the summer we moved from Virginia to California. I called the trip our three thousand mile obstacle course.

Our first obstacle was our car. We were driving an old Volkswagen that left a trail of oil from one coast to the other. Inside that little car were two parents, two children, one cat, and one dog (who weren't the best of friends), an array of suitcases, games, books, toys, snacks, and, of course, a case of oil. We towed an even older Volkswagen Bug. It had once been all yellow until an accident gave it two red fenders. We were a bright parade.

The moving van had left, and the car was loaded so we all piled into the car and were off. We got clear to the end of our driveway before we made our first stop. That's when the dog jumped out the window to chase the neighbor's cat. Then the kids jumped out to chase the dog, and then the parents jumped out to chase the kids. The only smart one in the car was the cat who jumped out to run away. We finally retrieved the dog, the cat, and the kids, and we were on our way again.

The obstacles had begun. Some of them were small, like being a house guest in a home where their dog hated our cat. Then there were the rest stops where the dog wouldn't get out of the car, and the cat wouldn't get back in. (Incidentally, if you ever thought about training your cat to walk on a leash, don't bother.)

Then there were the bigger obstacles, like driving through a record heat wave in a car that was not air conditioned. We planned to overcome the heat by reversing that silly habit of driving during the day and sleeping at night. Instead, we slept during the day and drove at night. The plan worked well until our car broke down in Emporia, Kansas, at 1:30 a.m. Guess how many mechanics are on duty in Emporia, Kansas, at 1:30 in the morning. Then there was the tire that went flat during a rain storm. Then there was a new transmission in Albuquerque. I only hope that the driver of the tow truck thought that having the four of us, plus the dog and cat, in his cab was as much fun as we did.

Our three thousand mile obstacle course turned out to be an experience that I wouldn't trade for anything, nor take anything to repeat. The trip taught me that God doesn't always remove obstacles from our pathway. Sometimes he leaves them there to teach us to rely on him (2 Corinthians 1:8–9).

I'm praying to be a quick learner! Aren't you?

Who Me, Lost?

I get lost a lot. Now, that's not only very inconvenient, but as my children grew old enough to tell their father how often it happened, it became downright embarrassing. It didn't come as a surprise to him, however. He had already discovered that navigation was not my thing when, on our honeymoon, he handed me the map and asked how far it was to Chicago. After some deliberation I proudly announced, "About half an inch!"

But it was a discovery made too late for by now I was married into the Navy, which meant spending every other year of my life trying to find my way around some new place. Fortunately, I married a man who can get me to where I want to go.

Consider, for example, the trip we made to England to celebrate our twenty-fifth wedding anniversary. We had planned to share the driving, but I found driving on the left side of the street very confusing. I'm not saying that they drive on the wrong side of the street, but it certainly wasn't the right side. About half way through England, my husband decided that it would be best if he did all the driving while I did the navigating. You would think after twenty-five years of marriage he would know better. He soon remembered, however, and decided that a better plan was for me to just hold the map so he could navigate and drive at the same time.

I didn't mind being lost in England, but it's quite another thing to be lost in eternity. That's why I love the story Jesus told about the lost sheep in Luke 15. The story is about a shepherd who had a hundred sheep, but when he counted them, only ninety-nine were there. Then the shepherd goes out to look for the lost sheep. When he finds it, he "joyfully carries it home."

The lost sheep? That's you and me. The Good Shepherd who has come to bring us home? That's Jesus. We can say, "No thank you," if we don't want to go with him. But why anyone would rather be lost than found is beyond me.

A Heavenly Picnic

I love picnics. I hope you do too because when we get to heaven there are going to be a lot of picnics. At least, that's the thought that came to mind one day when I was out walking.

It works this way. In heaven, each of us will have a day set aside for a picnic in our honor, and there will be just one picnic a day. "That would take a long time," you say? Maybe, but in heaven, who's in a hurry?

Each picnic will be by invitation only. And when the day draws near for your picnic, invitations will be sent only to those who prayed for you. That means, of course, that you will be invited only to the picnics of the people you prayed for.

At your picnic, you will walk around being surprised and blessed to discover who is there. How lovely to be able to thank the people who prayed for you. And since Jesus has prayed for you (Romans 8:34), he will be there too. Just imagine being able to say, "Thank you," to Jesus! Your guests will be blessed too, because on that day they will discover how their prayers for you were answered. Remember all those prayers we thought were to no avail? This is the day when we discover how the Lord used them.

Just a dream? Maybe, but I am convinced that in some special way we will know who prayed for us. Likewise, in some special way, those who prayed for us will know how their prayers were answered.

Every now and then I look at someone and offer a prayer for that person. Then I find myself thinking, *Now I get to come to your picnic!*

Wouldn't you like to come to mine?

What Will People Think?

In high school, my classmates could hardly wait until class was over to find my older brother and tell him what dumb question his sister had just asked. My poor brother! Not only my questions, but my jokes were the bane of his existence as if he, older and wiser by a whole year, was responsible for my education.

As I grew older and supposedly wiser, I eventually learned that sophisticated people aren't supposed to ask questions that show their ignorance. And since I wanted people to think I was as smart and sophisticated as the next guy, I learned that the only question that really mattered was, "What will people think?"

It's a question that Jesus never asked, but I bet his disciples did. Consider, for example, the time Jesus called the Pharisees "snakes" and "vipers" (Matthew 23:33). Can't you hear the disciples saying, "Jesus, you've got to stop talking like that. What will people think?"

At the very least, Jesus could have just kept quiet, but he wouldn't do that either. Nor was he particular with whom he talked. He even talked with sinners, and everyone knows you're not supposed to do that. After all, "What will people think?"

Then there was his trial with all the important people in Jerusalem asking him just who he thought he was. Now he chooses to say scarcely a word. Jesus certainly could have used a good PR man. But Jesus would have none of it because Jesus didn't come to impress us; he came to save us.

Well, what people think about us really doesn't matter. Nor does it matter what we think about other people. It does matter, however, what we think about the One who said, *"I am the way and the truth and the life. No one comes to the Father except through me"* (John 14:6).

If Jesus is right, and I think he is, then your answer to the question, "Is Jesus *your* way, *your* truth and *your* life?" has eternal consequences.

Are you ready to answer yes or are you hesitating because of what people might think?

Facing the Lions

Alfred Lord Tennyson once wrote, "More things are wrought by prayer than this world dreams of." And no one's prayers wrought more than did those of a man named Daniel.

Daniel is best known as the man who spent a night in the lions' den and lived to tell about it. Today's news media probably would have run a headline that said something like, "Man Rejected by Lions." By the time you finished reading the story, you'd be feeling sorry for those poor hungry lions.

The lions may have ignored Daniel, but God did not. When Daniel prayed, God listened. One day I made the mistake of telling the Lord that I wanted to pray like Daniel. I tried to discover Daniel's formula for successful prayer until the Lord said, "Marjorie, prayer is not a formula; it is a lifestyle. If you want to pray like Daniel, you have to *be* like Daniel."

"*Be* like Daniel? Lord, you've got to be kidding." The Bible describes Daniel as "intelligent" and "well-informed," with a "keen mind," able "to interpret dreams, explain riddles, and solve diffi-cult problems." He was "neither corrupt nor neg-ligent" (Daniel 1–6). To top it off, an angel called him "highly esteemed" not once, not twice, but three times (9:23; 10:11,19).

I was ready to follow in Daniel's footsteps. "Lord, bring on those visions, dreams, and angels." Then the thought entered my mind, *Don't forget the lions!* To be quite honest, that idea was more appealing when Daniel was in the palace than when he was in the lions' den. If angels and lions are a package deal, I may need to give this more thought.

Whether I know it or not, the truth is that I do live near a dangerous lion. So do you. The Bible calls him "the devil" and describes him as an enemy who "prowls around like a roaring lion looking for some-one to devour" (I Peter 5:8).

With the roaring lion closing in to devour us, who does God send to save us but a defenseless Lamb. The lion has sharp fangs and claws; the Lamb has neither. Nevertheless, the Lamb steps between us and the devouring lion.

The Lamb died, and his body was placed in a

tomb. The tomb was closed by a huge stone. The lion thought that he had won.

Then God rolled away the stone—not to let the Lamb out, but to let us see that the tomb was already empty. The Lamb had won after all!

Father God, help us to know that there is a dangerous lion wanting to devour us. But there is also a Lamb wanting to bless us.

Choose carefully: a Lamb is a much better companion than a lion.

It's Easy to Be Nice on an Air Conditioned Bus

It's easy to be nice on an air conditioned bus. That was the thought that kept running through my mind as I trudged up the mountain in Jerusalem that was cleverly disguised as a city street. There were forty of us on a study tour in Israel, and this was the hottest day since our arrival. The sun was directly overhead and merciless. Even worse, we were late for lunch. I kept glancing over my shoulder, hoping to see our air conditioned bus coming to pick us up, but it never came. I was learning that it is not so easy to be nice when I'm only halfway up the hill, it's hot, and I'm hungry and tired.

I thought of the people in Exodus who were also hot, hungry, and tired. What if it had happened today? Would today's conveniences have changed the outcome? My imagination went to work.

I imagined Moses boarding a plane to Cairo. As his plane stops at the gate, he pulls out his cell phone and calls Pharaoh's office for an appointment. Since everyone is in a meeting, Moses leaves a voicemail.

When Pharaoh hears Moses say, "Let my people go," it makes him angry. Pharaoh tells his secretary, "Call that man back and tell him that not only am I not going to let them go, but I'm going to make them work harder than before."

The next morning Moses opens the morning paper and reads the following, "Construction Budget Cut. The state is no longer able to provide straw to the brick makers. We are sorry for the inconvenience, but the brick makers will now have to provide their own materials."

Some of the brick makers picket. Others, however, hop into their pickup trucks and head to Home Depot. They buy the straw they need and charge it to Moses.

Meanwhile, Moses and Pharaoh are negotiating God's demand. Pharaoh continues to refuse to let the people go until the night of the big standoff. Pharaoh loses! He sends an e-mail to Moses@God. com. The message simply says, "Go!" Their suitcases packed, the Israelites head out towards the desert, singing and dancing.

It doesn't take long, however, before they find themselves hot, thirsty, and tired. Fortunately, Moses has negotiated a contract with the Promised Land Bus Company to meet them at the border with a huge fleet of air conditioned buses stocked with enough bottled water to take them across the desert. Whoever got the contract to provide several million people with bottled water would quickly become wealthy. That is until their competitor files a lawsuit charging them with monopolizing the market.

The Israelites settle down in their comfortable seats in the cool bus. They eat their box lunches while watching CNN Headline News. A news flash shows Pharaoh telling a reporter that he has changed his mind and has sent the army to bring them back. CNN, of course, will be on the scene to bring their viewers details of the battle.

Then the reporter asks Moses, "You are caught between the Red Sea and the Egyptian army. What will you do?"

Moses answers, "We will cross the Red Sea ... No, it is not my crazy idea ... No, I do not intend to file an environmental impact statement."

Well, back to reality as I have finally reached the

top of the hill. Would the story have ended any differently if they had the resources of the twenty-first century? I don't think so because the problem wasn't their resources—but their hearts. Our resources have changed over the years, but not our hearts. Their hearts were sinful and got them into trouble. They still do today.

But God desires to change our hearts. "I will give you a new heart and put a new spirit in you; I will remove from you your heart of stone and give you a heart of flesh" (Ezekiel 36:26).

Do you have your new heart yet?

Computers Don't Take Turns

We have a new pet at our house. It's a mouse, and so far it has been training me far more than I have been training it. My training has taught me, among other things, to manage the mouse, drag the mouse, clean the mouse, and even how to make mouse trails.

All of this means, of course, that we now have a computer. The computer reminds me a lot of our other pet, a dog, because neither one of them does what I want. At least the computer doesn't demand to go out in the middle of the night.

But the computer does have demands. For example, it demands that I do things its way. It demands that I follow its rules. Rules are frustrating for someone like me who thinks that the money machine should give me most of my money if I remember most of my PIN. I have learned, instead, that unless I am absolutely right, I get absolutely nothing.

The computer also demands that I do things its way all the time. But I think computers should have a "my turn" key. When I click that key, it would be my turn to make the rules. I would use it only when I am totally frustrated, which shouldn't be more than once every three or four minutes.

Frustrating as it is, I am still the computer's willing pupil because it enables me to do things that I enjoy. For example, with my *CreataCard* software, I can make wonderful greeting cards and pretend that I'm creative. With my *Bible Explorer* software, I can study and pretend that I know more of the Bible than I can remember. And with *Word,* I can make corrections without whiteout and pretend that I don't make mistakes.

Some days I think how nice it would be if people were more like the computer. For example, if we had an "undo" key we could take back the last thing we did or said. And we wouldn't have senior moments because we would just get a new memory chip.

But there are many more days when I am so grateful that people are not more like computers. My computer makes a terrible friend because it doesn't care about me. For example, although I've spent hours learning about the computer, the computer has never learned a thing about me, nor does it want to. Computers are user-neutral; they don't care who the user is. Anyone who knows the password and the rules can use its services.

Computers never ask how my day was because it makes no difference to them. They don't make it easier if I've had a bad day. They don't make it harder if they don't like me. They never smile, hug, pat me on the back. And though it's true that they tell some good jokes, they never laugh with me.

Lord, I am so glad that my friends are not like my computer. I thank you that they do care, that they do ask how I am, that they do smile when they see me, and that some have even been known to laugh at my jokes.

Help all of us to be true friends to those you have placed in our lives.

You Forgot What?

Forgetfulness can be very embarrassing, like the time I called the doctor to make an appointment for my newborn. It seemed like a simple enough question when the nurse asked if I had a boy or a girl, but I couldn't remember. That was embarrassing!

Another embarrassing experience was the time I volunteered to help drive some Boy Scouts home from summer camp. When we got back home, and the boys had taken all of their stuff out of my car, there was one sleeping bag left. One sleeping bag too many meant one boy too few.

Where was he? I had forgotten him. He was still at camp. So I had to tell his waiting parents that the sleeping bag was here, but not the boy. They probably didn't consider that a fair trade off. Then again, maybe they did.

We spend a lot of energy remembering things that we don't want to forget. Consider weddings, for example. Can't you see the mother of the bride running back and forth with a list in her hand of things she mustn't forget to do? Nevertheless, something is always forgotten.

But I bet there is one thing that has never been forgotten at any wedding, at any time, or at any place. Imagine, if you will, the bride walking down the aisle on the arm of her proud father. The bride looks to the right and smiles. She looks to the left and smiles. Then she looks down, and she gasps; she is still dressed in her jeans and t-shirt—she had forgotten to put on her wedding dress.

Wouldn't you agree that to forget such a thing is absurd? Yet God says that his people have forgotten something even more absurd: they have forgotten him! "Does a young woman forget her jewelry? Does a bride hide her wedding dress? No! Yet for years on end my people have forgotten me" (Jeremiah 2:32, NLT).

Thank you, Father, that you do not forget us. Please enable us to return the favor.

There Goes the Neighborhood

It is one thing to invite Jesus Christ into your heart, but it's quite another thing to invite him into your neighborhood. His presence could be costly.

For example, notice in the New Testament that wherever Jesus went, a crowd of people went after him. Although from time to time he sought to get away from them, more often than not he welcomed them. Surely you've noticed that large crowds make a lot of noise. And they are so, well, messy.

Remember when he fed the five thousand? It's a terrific story, but I'm glad that he didn't do it in my backyard. All those people would really wreck my lawn. They might even pick some of my flowers. Who do you suppose would pay for all that damage?

Oh, dear! There's Jesus knocking on my front door. It's raining now, and he wants to bring some of those people inside. Isn't there somewhere else they can go for the evening teaching? What if they go into my living room? Surely they won't sit on my antique chairs! And if that isn't bad enough, remember the New Testament account where some fellows cut a hole in the roof in order to lower their sick friend in to see Jesus (Mark 2:4). What if they tried that on my house? Who do you suppose would pay for all that damage?

Nothing was safe. Once, Jesus sent demons into a herd of pigs and sent them off a cliff to their death. That story doesn't worry me; I don't own any pigs. I don't own any fig trees either (Matthew 21:18–19). But if I did, who do you suppose would pay for all that damage?

If you really want a neighbor who won't bother you, don't invite Jesus; invite a Pharisee. They won't bother you. In fact, they won't even talk to you, and they most certainly won't be knocking on your door. Pharisees considered themselves superior beings, and they didn't mind who knew it.

I'm glad that Jesus was not like the Pharisees. I am glad that he came into neighborhoods like mine and talked with people like me. Maybe I shouldn't worry about the damage. After all, it cost him a whole lot more than it cost me.

A Sense of Humor Helps

If you haven't developed a sense of humor by the time you're sixty, you're in trouble. That thought came to mind a few weeks ago when I opened my purse to pay for groceries, only to discover everything floating in iced tea with a lemon on top. Iced tea doesn't do much for a check book, but fortunately the credit card still worked. (Since then, I've done a better job of tightening the lid on my iced tea glass.)

A sense of humor helps not only with our small problems, but also with our big ones. I have a big one called Parkinson's disease. It just appeared at my door some years ago and walked right in, completely uninvited. It's one of those anniversaries I count but don't celebrate.

Invited or not, it seems that it has settled in for awhile, so I'm learning to deal with it. My primary symptom is not the typical tremor, but something called freezing. In Parkinson's, freezing doesn't mean being cold. It means being unable to move, like a ship frozen in ice. When it happens, I can't lift my feet off the floor, and let me tell you, not being able to lift your feet off the floor does make it difficult to walk.

Freezing is very embarrassing because it tends to happen in the most inconvenient places, like doorways. It's especially embarrassing when others want to go through the doorway too, but can't because I'm in the way. To get my feet moving, I have developed some fancy footwork that my son describes as my roadrunner windup. If you have ever watched the Roadrunner cartoon, you get the picture. I have decided, however, that not being able to start is a whole lot better than not being able to stop.

Besides being embarrassing, freezing can be downright annoying. In small places, like kitchens, that require constant turning around, I soon feel like a ballerina in combat boots.

I have a perfect plan for solving that problem. It's called, Let's Eat Out! However, my patient husband, who already takes me out to dinner so often that he's thinking of selling the kitchen, says that he has the perfect plan—roller skates.

All of this isn't to say that Parkinson's is to be taken lightly. It is not! It is a serious affliction that I didn't choose. The only real choice I have is how to react to it. I can become bitter, or I can allow God to use it to make me better. In my book, better wins over bitter any day. I won't ask if you have difficulties in your life. Of course you do! But I will ask this: are your trials making you better or bitter?

Computers and Children

"Computers are just wonderful," everyone says.

"They save so much time."

They may be wonderful, I thought to myself, *but I've not noticed that they save any time. To the contrary, they seem to absorb man hours like a dry sponge dropped into water.*

They are a lot like children that way. In fact, in the time we've had our home computer, I've noticed a variety of similarities between computers and children. For example:

- They both weigh in at just a few pounds, but the entire household soon revolves around them.

- The space they require expands.

- So does the time.

- They both insist that things be done their way, and life can be very unpleasant until they get it.

- Their initial purchase price isn't too bad, but there is no end to the accessories they can't do without.

- They both generate a lot of mess, and I've noticed that neither of them ever picks up after themselves.

- They both store up endless amounts of useless information.

- It can be very difficult to get either of them to work.

- They both require more patience than I ever hope to have.

- In no time at all, I found myself wondering what I ever did without them.

In spite of their similarities, however, computers and children are not the same. After all, computers are things; children are people. Life works best when we remember to use things and love people. It never works well the other way around.

Is life working well for you?

Getting to Know All About You

If you really want to get to know someone, travel with them. Of course, if you really don't want them to get to know you, you'd better stay home. Exodus tells of the time God offered to take the Israelites from Egypt back to Israel. The Israelites probably should have stayed in Egypt!

But they agreed, and off they went on what they thought would be a grand adventure. Their joy didn't last long, however, because they soon found themselves trapped between the Red Sea and the Egyptian army. What would they do? Would they remember their miraculous delivery from Egypt and trust God to deliver them again? Not a chance! They were terrified. So they responded by doing what they did best: they complained.

Their complaining was soon replaced by jubilation, however, because they saw that the Red Sea didn't stop God. It didn't stop them either, once God divided the waters. It did, however, stop the Egyptians.

Once again, their jubilation lasted until the next crisis. Once again they responded by doing what they did best: they complained. In fact, they never stopped complaining.

Eventually, God decided that he'd had enough, so he said something like this to Moses, "I've had it with these people of yours whom you brought out of Egypt. I'm out of here."

Moses knew these people too, so he spoke right up and said something like this to God: "No way! Remember, Lord, this was your idea, not mine. These are your people, not mine. You are the one who brought them out of Egypt—not me" (Exodus 33:1- 13).

"Then Moses pleaded, 'If your presence does not go with us, do not send us from here'" (verse 15). Verse 17 tells us that God relented.

The Israelites made the mistake of thinking that God's presence would make their journey easy. But Moses, who had traveled with God before, knew that God wouldn't make their journey easy, only possible.

What do you think about traveling with God?

Have you learned to trust him through the hard days and to thank him for the good days?

Do you ever wonder what he thinks about traveling with you?

My Forever Friend

I'm good at moving. Most navy wives are. That's because we get a lot of practice, and you know the saying, "Practice makes perfect." I won't bother you with the names of all of the places we've lived or visited, but they cover a fair amount of the globe.

There is nothing new about moving. The Bible tells us that it began shortly after Creation when Adam and Eve moved out of their garden apartment because they were in trouble with their landlord.

Then there was Noah. Noah lived in a "corrupt and violent" neighborhood (Genesis 6:11), so God told him to get ready for a move. Only it wasn't Noah who moved away from the neighborhood; it was the neighborhood that moved away from Noah.

Then there was Abraham's move, prompted by the Lord telling him something like, "Go west, young man. Go west." So Abraham went home and packed the suitcases. Sarah might have felt better about it if she only knew where they were going.

Here we are in the twenty-first century, and we are still moving. I asked God if he ever thought to design us with wheels instead of feet. He didn't seem to think that it was nearly as good an idea as I did. Maybe he thinks we move fast enough as it is.

Moving is a lot of trouble. But it brings a lot of blessings too. Without a doubt, my greatest blessing has been the wonderful people we have met.

Likewise, the most difficult part of moving is leaving those friends behind. It is very lonely to find yourself surrounded by people you don't know and who don't know you.

Well, someday God will tell me it is time to make one last move, this time into his presence. But I won't go as a stranger because God already knows my name. I won't get lost because his Son came to be my path. I won't be locked out, because his Son came to be my door. I won't be afraid because his Son came to be my shepherd. And I won't be in darkness because his Son came to be my light.

God's Son is Jesus. Jesus is my forever friend.

He will be yours too. You only have to ask.

The Best Is Yet to Be

The TV commercial said, "You're not getting older; you're getting better." All I had to do, they said, was use their product to color my hair, and I would be immediately transformed from older to better.

Don't I wish! But a quick glance in the mirror told me that it was going to take more than hair color to hide the fact that I was, indeed, getting older. Besides that, there were plenty of other clues, and I couldn't hide them all.

For example, one day I opened my mailbox and found that AARP had sent me an application for membership. *Why are they inviting me?* I thought. *Isn't AARP for old people?* Then Medicare and Social Security notified me that I was eligible for their services. *That can't be right,* I thought. *Those are programs for the elderly.* Besides that, I no longer have to ask for a senior discount; one look, and they automatically give it to me!

Even my husband, who is older than I am, hasn't been silent on the subject. For example, when our first grandchild was born, he loudly announced that he was too young to be married to a grandmother! I returned the favor when he went on Medicare.

Then last summer, when he was driving our new Honda, he commented, "This is probably the last car we will buy." You have to remember that this is the man who keeps his cars next-to-forever. Anyway, that was okay with me because it would take me that long to figure out how to turn on the windshield wipers.

However, his most memorable comment about getting older came one day when he was praying, "Lord, bless our aging parents." He suddenly stopped, looked up at me and exclaimed, "We are the aging parents!"

Is getting older really so bad? Consider what Robert Browning wrote in his poem, Rabbi ben Ezra:

> Grow old along with me! The best is yet to be,
> The last of life, for which the first was made:
> Our times are in His hand, Who saith,

'A whole I planned, Youth shows but
half; trust God: see all, nor be afraid!

I'm trusting God that the best is yet to be. Does
anybody want my hair color kit?

God's Not Nice

Have you ever read a book called *God's Not Nice*? I haven't either, but I think one needs to be written because it's a side of God that we need to consider. Such a book obviously requires a definition of the word *nice*. My dictionary defines nice as "agreeable, charming, friendly, Jim-dandy, and pleasant." These words can describe one side of God, although I'd probably stop short of Jim-dandy. But to limit him to these words is to miss another side of his character.

Consider, for example, what he did to Jeremiah. God called Jeremiah to be a prophet and then sent him to Jerusalem, a city well known for killing prophets. God gave Jeremiah a message for them, and then told him they would not listen to him, but he was to tell them anyway. Then, knowing the danger Jeremiah would face, God said, "They will fight against you but will not overcome you, for I am with you and will rescue you."

So where was God when Jeremiah was beaten and put in the stocks in Jeremiah 20:2? Where was God when Jeremiah was beaten and put in a dungeon in Jeremiah 37:15–16? And where was God when Jeremiah was left to starve to death in the bottom of a deep cistern in Jeremiah 38:6, 9? I ask you, was that nice of God to say, "I will protect you," and then let these things happen?

Jeremiah reminds me of a scene in a Tarzan movie I saw some years ago. In the scene was a man trying to cross over a deep canyon on a bridge made of rotting rope. With each step, another strand of the rope broke. When the last strand broke, the bridge fell and so did the man. He would have been dashed to pieces on the rocks below except that Tarzan swooped down on his magic vine and saved him.

Now Jeremiah was on a bridge like that because God put him there. And it seems to me that a nice God, one who is "agreeable, delightful, and charming," would say, "Now don't you worry, Jeremiah. I will secure the bridge until you are safely across to the other side." But God never promised Jeremiah that the bridge wouldn't break. What God did promise was to catch him before he landed on the sharp rocks below.

Well, life hasn't changed much over the centuries. We like to think that in Christ our troubles are now over, and life will be "agreeable, delightful, and charming." But Jesus didn't come to make us nice; he came to make us good. And this is the message he left us, "In this world you will have trouble. But take heart! I have overcome the world" (John 16:33).

Where Did You Go, God?

A Primer on How Not to Pray

Good morning, Lord.

Did you sleep well? I don't have much time to pray this morning, so I'm wondering if I get extra credit for kneeling.

Lord, I know there are some things I promised to do for you today, but can they possibly wait until the end of the week? You have seen my busy calendar, and I'm sure you understand.

In the meantime, could you do just a couple of things for me? My boss will be at the meeting this morning, as will be Ms. Fisher. Would it be too much to ask you to keep Ms. Fisher from being her usual self? Where does she get all those questions from anyway? You know, Lord, it would help me a lot if you would just move her to the Cincinnati office.

You've mentioned something about wanting to cleanse my heart, but we've never scheduled it. Will it take long? I would be most appreciative if we could avoid the weekends. Instead, how about Tuesdays and Thursdays between four and six p.m.? That way I could still make it to my bowling league by six thirty.

May I remind you that this Sunday is my big lawn party? I am sure you understand why I can't make it to church. There is one problem: it's supposed to rain! I know that the farmers really need rain, but can't they wait until Monday? You know how my hair looks when it is so humid outside.

Well, Lord, that's about it for this morning. Oh, just one more thing. Yesterday I asked for a close parking space. Well, three blocks isn't exactly close! Do you think you could do better today?

Did you say something, God? I know the TV is loud, but my program is almost over.

What was that? Thunder! Funny, the paper didn't mention that a storm was on the way.

The Grumble Seat

God must have had a smile on his face when he created dogs and cats. We had a dog named Linus and a cat named Lucy who certainly made us smile. In fact, they provided the comic relief for our family. That was especially true when we made long car trips.

For example, our dog, Linus, loved every minute of every mile. We referred to him as the sheriff because he was always on patrol. For Linus, each new day meant new horizons, new adventures, and a new motel. Our only problem with Linus was that he never wanted to get out of the car.

But our cat Lucy hated every minute of every mile in the car, and she was not quiet about it. Lucy gave us a lot of problems, one of which was getting her back into the car and then back into her cage. Do you know how to get a spread–eagled cat into a cage? Backwards.

When the time came to move, I wanted to take Linus and Lucy in the car with us. I knew that Linus was not a problem. I also knew that Lucy, who didn't like the car, would be. But I had hoped that she would adapt. Ha! What was I thinking? Cats do not adapt. No indeed! Cats make loud, wailing noises when they are unhappy. I thought for sure that she would either quiet down or develop laryngitis, neither of which ever happened.

Then one morning, I looked at the car we were towing and had one of my rare moments of brilliance. Cars once had a rumble seat. Why couldn't we have a grumble seat? If we couldn't mute her, we could move her. So we stopped and moved her to the car we were towing. We immediately crowned her the *Queen of Grumble*, and the towed car became her kingdom.

Actually, no one likes to be around grumblers, including God (Numbers 11:1). Maybe all of us would be better company if we joined Oswald Chambers in his prayer, "Lord, may you not find the whine in us any more, but may you find us ready to face anything you bring."

Choose Wisely

The English language is so illogical. We say, for example, that we park on the driveway and drive on the parkway. Wouldn't it be more logical to say that we park on the parkway and drive on the driveway? Logical or not, that's how it is.

People are illogical too. Suppose you were offered an awesome place where you could live as long as you wanted to, rent free. All you had to do was not eat the fruit that was in the refrigerator. Wouldn't it be logical to leave the fruit alone?

Adam and Eve's Landlord made them an offer like that, and they took it. They were doing a pretty good job of leaving the fruit alone until some fast talker came by and suggested otherwise. Curiosity got the best of Eve, and she took a bite. Then she offered a taste to Adam, who no doubt mumbled something like, "Yes, dear," before he took a bite. We've all had indigestion ever since.

If people are illogical, then so are nations. A nation, after all, is just a group of people united by a common tax system. Consider, for example, the ancient Israelites who decided that 430 years in Egypt (Exodus 12:40–41) was long enough, and they wanted to go home. But Pharaoh, who thought that he was in control, refused to let them go. Through a series of miracles, the God of Israel revealed that it was he who controlled night and day, heaven and earth, and life and death—not the Pharaoh.

So the Pharaoh let them go, but he quickly changed his mind and sent his army to bring them back. Soon the Israelites were trapped between the Red Sea and the advancing army. But seas are not a problem for God; after all, he created them. He just opened this one for the Israelites to walk through. The army was not a problem either. God just closed the sea and washed them away.

Three days after walking through the "walls of water," the Israelites got thirsty. Wouldn't you think they had seen enough to know that God could be trusted for a glass of water? Not a chance! They preferred to grumble; it was a habit they never relinquished.

We are all used to illogical behavior from people. But do we ever think of God as being illogical? If not, consider this from John 3:16:

For God so loved the world
Is it logical that a righteous God should
love people like you and me?

that he gave his one and only Son
Is it logical that he would send his beloved
Son to be our Passover lamb?

that whoever believes in him
Is it logical that he would allow us to
ignore both the Gift and the Giver?

shall not perish, but have eternal life.
The stakes are high!
It is logical to choose wisely.

Have you?

Minor vs. Major

You know the difference between minor and major surgery, don't you? Surgery is minor when it happens to someone else; it is major when it happens to you. But I think we can all agree that whenever a surgeon is standing over someone's brain with a scalpel in his hand that it is *major*.

I just had brain surgery. Its purpose was to bring relief to a problem that began, strangely enough, in my left foot. That was seventeen years ago, and that tremor in my left foot was the unrecognizable beginning of Parkinson's disease.

Heaven knows that I've prayed often enough for God to take it away. So have those who pray better than I do. But God has not answered those prayers. Although I wish he would, I don't believe that God has ever promised to heal everyone in this life. I know that is controversial, but nevertheless, that is what I think.

What he has promised, however, is that he will never leave us nor forsake us (Hebrews 13:5). He has also promised that he will always provide a way of escape so that we can endure (1 Corinthians 10:13). And that is what he has been teaching me—to endure. This has been my experience with Parkinson's; every time it progresses to a point that I think is unbearable, God shows up and reveals some new thing that enables me to endure.

This surgery was an example of that. It is called DBS, which stands for Deep Brain Stimulation. It does not cure, but it does minimize some of the symptoms of Parkinson's like not being able to walk. And that was where I was headed until this surgery. If you are looking for someone who walks normally, you have to look further than me. But if you are looking for someone who can walk; well, here I am.

If you have a burden that you cannot be rid of, you can keep asking God to remove it. If it persists, however, perhaps you must endure it. Whatever the size of that burden, I pray that God will strengthen you with his glorious power so that you will have all the patience and endurance that you need (Colossians 1:11).

May God bless us all as we struggle with the difficulties in our lives.

CNN Interviews Mr. Noah

Good morning to you. This is your CNN reporter coming from the driveway of a man named Mr. Noah. We are here because Mr. Noah is building something that is as big as it is strange.

CNN: Tell me, sir, what is this big thing you are building in your driveway?

Noah: It's an ark.

CNN: A what?

Noah: An ark.

CNN: What's an ark?

Noah: It's something God told me to build.

CNN: Who?

Noah: God did.

CNN: Who's God?

Noah: He's the one who is going to send the rain.

CNN: What's rain?

Noah: It's how he's going to flood the earth.

CNN: Does this mean I'd better buy flood insurance?

Noah: I wouldn't bother.

CNN: Why is he going to flood the earth?

Noah: He told me the reason, but you won't like it.

CNN: Try me.

Noah: He says because "man only thinks of evil all the time, and he has filled the earth with corruption and violence."

CNN: Oh, I don't know that we are so bad. The movies are worse.

Noah: What's a movie?

Well, there it is, ladies and gentlemen. If Mr. Noah is right…What? Wait a minute. Something strange is happening. The air is getting wet. Could this be what he meant by rain? Bundle up, folks. It's going to be wet out there today!

The Ministry of Pixie Dust

My sister-in-law has what I call the ministry of pixie dust, and in the forty-nine years I've been married to her brother, I've seen her sprinkle it often. You do remember pixie dust, don't you? It's the golden dust that Tinker Bell, the diminutive fairy in Disney's *Peter Pan*, sprinkled on people, enabling them to fly.

I tell my sister-in-law that she is sprinkling pixie dust on people when she tells them about some good thing she saw them do. For example, I was helping her at a craft fair. When the fair was over, she went to the table next to us where a mom and her son were putting their things away. She said to the young boy, "I've been watching you help your mother for the past two hours, and I'd like to say how blessed she is to have such a patient, helpful son!" As she walked back to the table, I watched their faces. They didn't know it, but they were covered with gold!

It reminds me of the story told about the great evangelist Dwight Moody. The story says that one evening Mr. Moody boarded a train. Because it was so late in the evening, the car was almost empty. Nevertheless, an old man in shabby clothes stumbled into the seat right next to Mr. Moody. The old man pulled from his pocket a paper bag and with trembling hands proceeded to open the bag and then the bottle inside. He took a swig. Then, offering the bottle to Mr. Moody, he asked, "Would you like a drink?"

How would Mr. Moody, this man of God, this great evangelist, respond? I wondered what I would have done. Well, it seems that Mr. Moody carried pixie dust in his pocket too, and seeing this man through God's eyes, Mr. Moody replied, "No thank you, but how kind you are to offer to share with me something that is so important to you."

The old man's heart melted. Can't you hear Mr. Moody say, "May I share something with you that is very important to me?" He told the old gentleman about the gospel of Jesus Christ, and a new convert was soon welcomed into the Kingdom of God.

Is your pocket full of pixie dust? There is plenty to go around, so sprinkle away! The shortage isn't in its supply, but in its use.

Who Turned Off the Dark?

"It's getting dark out there," the minister said, as the sunlight streamed through the window. I thought he had lost his senses until I realized that he was talking about the spiritual, not the natural realm.

He continued, "The dictionary says that darkness is the absence of light." In other words, when you want a room to be dark, you don't go looking for the switch that turns on the dark; you look for the switch that turns off the light. If that's still not dark enough, you close the blinds and pull the drapes, not to keep the dark in, but to keep the light out.

Light is a wonderful thing. Adam and Eve were created to live in the light and to have fellowship with God. But their disobedience turned off that light, and men and women have lived in darkness ever since (Ephesians 6:12).

Jude verse 13 calls this kind of darkness the "blackest darkness." The first time I was in black darkness was when we were in West Virginia touring a coal mine. When we were deep inside the mine, the guide asked, "Do you want to see real darkness?" Then he turned the lights off. The dark was so black that I could not see even the movement of my hand in front of my face.

This darkness was not romantic. It did not make me want to sing "Some Enchanted Evening." This was total darkness without even the reflected light of the moon or stars to see by. When the light disappeared, so did all my reference points. I felt lost and abandoned. Then the guide turned off that black darkness by turning on the light.

Jesus is like that guide. Only Jesus did not come into our dark world to turn a light on for us; he came to be a light for us. "I am the light of the world. Whoever follows me will never walk in darkness, but will have the light of life" (John 8:12). Thank you, Father, that you have called us "out of darkness into your wonderful light" (1 Peter 2:9). May we be quick to follow.

Never Trust a Hungry Lion

I have traveled a lot over the years, but one trip stands out above them all—our African safari in Kenya. My husband and I stayed at a safari camp where we ate and slept in tents. It was so surreal that I had to keep reminding myself that this was not Disney World; this was real.

But it was hard to remember that we weren't in Disney World when we were lying in bed at night listening to tiny spider monkeys scampering across the canvas tent over our heads, hippopotamuses snorting as they came up from the water for air, and somewhere, a wart hog running through a pack of baboons.

We ate breakfast and lunch under the trees watching giraffes and gazelles on the horizon. A formal dinner was served in a huge tent. Since it was dark when dinner was over, we were not allowed to walk back to our sleeping tents alone. The first night our escort carried a flashlight and a big stick. I hoped the stick was big enough for whatever he might meet. The second night he carried a rifle instead of the stick. I didn't ask why he was carrying a rifle instead of a stick because I was afraid that he would tell me something that I really didn't want to know.

Each morning before sunrise, a driver would pick up the two of us in a Land Rover for our safari. The Land Rover had an open roof so that we could stand up and see without obstruction. We didn't follow a road hoping to see the animals. Instead, the driver would see something, and across the grasslands we would go. We saw cheetahs, elephants, lions, hyenas, water buffaloes, giraffes, jackals, antelopes, exotic birds, rhinos, hippos, and even a few crocodiles.

One morning, our driver saw a lion and started driving towards him. He drove closer, and closer, and closer until we were just a few feet away. It entered my mind that it would be a good idea for me to sit down. I wondered if I could figure out how to close the top before the lion figured out that it was open.

However, the lion was not the least bit interested in us. "How can that be?" I asked our driver.

He answered, "Look at his big stomach. He has

already eaten for the day, and a full lion is a contented lion. But if he's hungry, beware!"

I wondered what it would be like to meet a lion who is always hungry. The word terror came to mind. It gave new meaning to 1 Peter 5:8, "Your enemy the devil prowls around like a roaring lion looking for someone to devour."

Strangely enough, God sent a Lamb to defeat the lion. Stranger yet, the Lamb won (1 Peter 1:18–21).

Wouldn't you like to be at the Lamb's side before the lion is at yours?

Jack the Cat

I'd like to tell you about Jack. Jack is our cat whose unusual behavior has led us to suspect that he is really a dog cleverly disguised as a cat.

For example, cats usually run and hide when company comes, but not Jack. Jack, behaving like a dog, comes running over as if to say, "Hello. Here I am. Thanks for dropping by. What shall we do?"

Jack doesn't eat like a cat either. Cats nibble at their food and always leave some in their dish for their next snack. But dogs don't nibble; they gulp until their food is gone. Jack has a doglike appetite, and his dish is usually empty. I suspect that if he could speak one word it would be, "Refill!"

Well, Jack may be more like a dog than a cat, but he's certainly not like me. For example, Jack doesn't have to get dressed every morning. His only use for the computer is to sleep in front of or walk across it. He doesn't drive a car, although he thinks he could.

He doesn't do a lot of shopping, and, as far as I know, he doesn't have a credit card. I am glad he can't dial a phone. But I do wish he could open doors for himself because when they are closed he always wants to be on the other side.

But probably the biggest difference between Jack and me is our concept of time. I pay attention to time; Jack does not. I have a clock in every room. I wear a watch. I have a calendar on my desk. Although Jack doesn't have any of those things, he is never late. When you sleep twenty hours a day, time is not a big deal.

But time is a big deal to people. In fact, Ben Franklin called it "the stuff that life is made of." Although we can't see it, smell it, or touch it, a quick glance in a mirror is all we need to verify that time is real and that it is marching on. Perhaps you've already noticed that the older you get, the faster it marches!

Carl Sandburg called time "the coin of your life." He goes on to say, "It is the only coin you have, and only you can determine how to spend it." The Bible says that we will spend it to please either our "sinful nature" or the "Spirit." The first choice leads to "destruction." The second choice leads to "eternal life" (Galatians 6:7–8).

Choose carefully! A cat may have nine lives, but we have eternity—and that is forever.

Aren't Game Shows Fun?

Aren't game shows fun? They must be because millions of people watch them on TV. The appeal of game shows seems obvious; for giving the right answer you receive lots of lovely prizes.

God has a game plan too, but I don't think it will ever attract a wide audience. For example, on "Wheel of Fortune" when you give the right answer you receive gifts. But just suppose that instead of receiving a gift someone gets to take from you anything that they want.

Well, that's what happens when you answer God's question correctly; the next thing you know he comes right into your life and begins telling you what he wants you to give to him. The trouble is that he wants everything!

Remember those folks who gave the right answer

to God's question, "Will you follow me?" Abraham said yes and gave up the old homestead to live out of a suitcase in a foreign land. Moses didn't do any better when he said yes. He gave up power and wealth to go talk to sheep in the middle of nowhere. Samson said yes and forever after said no to barbers and nightcaps. Ruth said yes, and she had to turn in her passport. Then Daniel, who was supposed to be so smart, said yes and gave up wine and meat for water and carrots.

It doesn't get any better in the New Testament. Zaccheus' consent cost him megabucks, although he must have been glad to get off that limb. Paul said yes and gave up his head. Don't you think that's a bit much? Yet what Jesus gave up tops them all. When he said yes he gave up heaven to live with the likes of you and me.

You've got to admit that all that giving is a weird prize for winning. G. K. Chesterton was right when he wrote, "It's not that the Christian faith was tried and found wanting. Instead, it was found difficult and not tried."

Have you played any games lately?

Kids Say the Darndest Things

Kids Say the Darndest Things was a bestselling book by Art Linkletter based on his TV interviews with kids. He would ask them a variety of questions, but the one that produced the best answers was "What did your mother tell you *not* to say on television?"

I think it was so popular because we all have kids who say the darndest things. I know that my kids did. For example, one day our little boy came running to tell us that "The Lizard of Oz" was on TV. Another day, he was excited over his discovery of "atoms and neutrals." Then there was his announcement at the dinner table that he was no longer going to eat food that contained "adjectives."

But my children don't talk that way anymore because they aren't children any more. According to 1 Corinthians 13:11, that's the way it should be: "When I was a child, I talked like a child; I thought like a child, I reasoned like a child. When I became a man, I put childish ways behind me."

But some people keep their childish ways, like Archie Bunker from the TV sitcom *All in the Family*. Archie was the classic example of a man who never put his childish ways behind him. He continued to mishandle words, and truth was a word that never entered his vocabulary. If it did, he might have to admit that he was wrong, something that Archie Bunker would never do.

C. S. Lewis was the opposite of Archie Bunker; Lewis wanted to know the truth even when it meant admitting that he was wrong. In *Surprised by Joy*, he wrote of the night he changed his mind about God.

> You must picture me alone in that room in Magdalen, night after night, feeling whenever my mind lifted even for a second from my work, the steady, unrelenting approach of him whom I so earnestly desired not to

meet. That which I greatly feared had at last come upon me. In the Trinity term of 1929, I gave in and admitted that God was God, and knelt and prayed: perhaps, that night, the most dejected and reluctant convert in all England.

Following the truth led Lewis to the one who said, "I am the way and the truth and the life. No one comes to the Father except through me" (John 14:6). Apparently, if you want to go to heaven, you have to follow him. If you prefer, you can follow the yellow brick road, but it will only get you to Kansas.

Are you sure the road you are following is going where you want to go?

Late in Time

My favorite tour in Australia was called Late in Time because it featured a late night walk through a rainforest. The tour began when a small van picked up eight of us near Cairns and drove us to the rainforest. Once there, we drove to the end of the paved road, then to the end of the unpaved road. We were now deep within the forest.

We got out of the van into a pitch black darkness that was so dense I felt like I had run into a wall. I was so very grateful when our guide handed out flashlights and told us to follow him. Let me assure you that I was not thinking of wandering on alone.

As we started down the faint outline of a path, my mind demanded to know why it is that I sign up for such things. My imagination, inspired by the darkness, was busy producing scary things—tigers for one. I felt sure there weren't any tigers around, but the guide hadn't actually said as much. It was reassuring to see him at the front of the line. As we followed him, however, it dawned on me that he had the look of a runner, a fast runner. In fact, everyone looked fast. Being the slowest runner in a group being chased by a tiger, even an imaginary one, is not good!

Fascination, however, soon replaced fear. I was fascinated, for example, to see the laser-bright eyes of possums reflecting our guide's infrared light. I was fascinated by the tree kangaroo; I didn't even know there was such a thing, but there he stood on a branch about twenty feet off the ground, looking down at us while we stood there looking up at him.

By the time our walk was over, I had a new understanding of a rainforest, a new definition of darkness, and a new appreciation of light.

If you dread the darkness in your own life, let me tell you about the One who said, "I am the light of the world. Whoever follows me will never walk in darkness, but will have the light of life" (John 8:12).

His name is Jesus, and while it may be too dark for you to find him, it's never too dark for him to find you.

An Anchor or a Ball and Chain

I was pleasantly surprised when my husband recently said to me, "You are my home base, my anchor."

That's nice, I thought, *that he sees me as his anchor rather than as his ball and chain. Since I cost him a lot of money, I am glad to know that he is happy with his investment.*

His comment set me to thinking about the similarities and the differences between an anchor and a ball and chain. They are alike by definition: both are weights attached by a chain to an object. Yet they have profoundly different purposes. For example:

An anchor is helpful.	A ball and chain is harmful.
An anchor is chosen.	A ball and chain is commanded.
An anchor enables.	A ball and chain impedes.
An anchor keeps you safe.	A ball and chain keeps others safe.
An anchor secures.	A ball and chain punishes.
An anchor keeps you from drifting away.	A ball and chain keeps you from running away.

Matthew Henry wrote, "We are in this world as a ship at sea, tossed up and down, and in danger of being cast away. We need an anchor to keep us sure and steady."

Henry found his anchor in Hebrews 6:19, "This certain hope of being saved is a strong and trustworthy anchor for our souls, connecting us with God himself behind the sacred curtains of heaven" (TLB).

Whom have you chosen to be your anchor? Is

he sure and steady? Is he strong and trustworthy? Will he be able to keep your head above the stormy waves? Choose carefully; there are dark clouds on the horizon!

A Prayer for America

We come to you, Father, in repentance and shame
To confess that America has forgotten your name.

We thanked you for helping with a note in the mail:
"We'll call if we need you. In the meantime, farewell."

We once promised God that we'd trust and obey.
But now we insist that we have our own way.

We call entertainment the things you call sin,
Then ask why our children find conflict within.

You say there is joy in our service to man.
Instead we acquire all the things that we can.

We take all our leisure doing what we want,
Pretending that next week we'll ask you what you
want.

Our planes own the skies. Our ships own the seas.
We're proud that we're standing and not on our
knees.

But things are not going as well as we planned.
We forgot that not all things are measured by man.

We forgot that you told us that you're not impressed
With power, or riches, or fame.

The nations we see whose plans are still blessed
Are the ones who have honored your name.

We honor your name when we trust and obey,
When we want what you want and not our own
way.

We're tall when we kneel and not when we stand,
Forgive us our sins, Lord. Please come, heal our
land!

*I wrote this poem after the tragedy of 9/11. I hope
you will pray it with me.

The Kneeling Santa

Mirrors are a quiet reflection of the fact that we are getting older. Our children tell us the same thing, but they're not known for being quiet about it. There was a time, however, when it wasn't in my children's noise, but in their silence that I heard my time clock loudly ticking away.

It happened one Christmas morning some years ago. Previously, our boisterous sons were always out of bed before sunrise, eager to see what presents Santa had brought for them. My husband and I would send them back to their rooms, hoping for a few more minutes of sleep. We were never successful, but every year we continued to try.

But on this Christmas morning the strangest thing happened. My husband and I woke up first. Our sons were still asleep. We dressed. They were still quiet. We had breakfast. They didn't make a sound! We rattled the packages. Still, no one stirred.

Eventually they did wake up. Eventually the presents were opened. And eventually it dawned on me that our children were getting older. And if they were getting older, then so were we. If any of you know a way for the children to get older while the parents don't, I wish you'd let me know, and the sooner the better.

Well, ages aren't the only things that change in a household; so do priorities. I recently saw a figurine showing Santa reverently kneeling before the baby Jesus that reminded me of how Christmas priorities have changed in our home. Before you decide which is first in your home, consider these differences:

Santa has a prearranged schedule and is always on time. He does not like to be noticed. Jesus, however, has the uncomfortable habit of ignoring all prearranged schedules. He shows up, instead, at the most unexpected times insisting that we not only notice him, but that we introduce him to our friends. He can be very embarrassing.

Santa wants the flue left open so he can come down the chimney. We always leave food for him, although there is no record of his ever having asked for any. Jesus, however, wants to come right in the front door. He brings food for me and offers to stay and share it.

Santa brings presents for those who have been good. He carries lumps of coal for those who have been bad. Jesus brings presents so we can be good. He carries no coal.

Santa gives me what I want. Jesus says that I must give up what I want.

Santa leaves right away. He wants nothing in return. Jesus, however, wants to stay. And he does want something: he wants the key to my heart.

I remember how often we had treated Santa as if he were God, and how often we had treated God as if he were Santa. The first part of our lives we had it wrong. The last part of our lives we hope to get it right.

You know, maybe getting older isn't so bad after all!

listen|imagine|view|experience

AUDIO BOOK DOWNLOAD INCLUDED WITH THIS BOOK!

In your hands you hold a complete digital entertainment package. Besides purchasing the paper version of this book, this book includes a free download of the audio version of this book. Simply use the code listed below when visiting our website. Once downloaded to your computer, you can listen to the book through your computer's speakers, burn it to an audio CD or save the file to your portable music device (such as Apple's popular iPod) and listen on the go!

How to get your free audio book digital download:

1. Visit www.tatepublishing.com and click on the e|LIVE logo on the home page.
2. Enter the following coupon code:
   cb0a-6449-5f6b-1c04-de1d-abc4-d83c-bf02
3. Download the audio book from your e|LIVE digital locker and begin enjoying your new digital entertainment package today!